Mastering the Art of Filet Mignon

A Comprehensive Cookbook

AF416012

While every precaution has been taken in the preparation of this book, the publisher assumes no responsibility for errors or omissions, or for damages resulting from the use of the information contained herein.

MASTERING THE ART OF FILET MIGNON

First edition. March 14, 2024.

Copyright © 2024 Jose Maria.

ISBN: 979-8224518524

Written by Jose Maria.

Table of Contents

Mastering the Art of Filet Mignon 1

Chapter (1) Selecting and Preparing Filet Mignon 3

Chapter (2) Essential Cooking Techniques 6

Chapter (3) Mouthwatering Recipes 9

Chapter (4) Sides and Accompaniments 18

Chapter (5) Tips and Techniques for Perfection 22

Chapter (6) Beyond the Basics 24

Chapter (7) Sides and Accompaniments (continued) 26

Chapter (8) Tips and Techniques for Perfection (continued) 30

Chapter (9) Special Occasion Recipes 32

Chapter (10) Healthier Alternatives and Dietary Considerations 37

Chapter (11) Family-Friendly Filet Mignon 40

Chapter (12) Holiday and Celebration Menus 42

Chapter (13) Filet Mignon Appetizers and Small Bites 45

Chapter (14) Global Filet Mignon Variations 49

Chapter (15) Filet Mignon Desserts 52

Chapter (16) Preserving and Repurposing Filet Mignon 54

Chapter (17) Filet Mignon Cooking Challenges 56

Chapter (18) Filet Mignon for Entertaining 58

Chapter (19) Sustainable Filet Mignon Practices 60

Chapter (20) Filet Mignon Garnishes and Flair 62

Jose Maria

❖ Introduction to Filet Mignon

A. What is Filet Mignon?

Filet mignon, pronounced "fee-lay min-yawn," is a highly prized and tender cut of beef that comes from the smaller end of the tenderloin muscle, which runs along the spine of the cow. Known for its exceptional tenderness and melt-in-your-mouth texture, filet mignon is often regarded as one of the most luxurious cuts of beef available.

B. History and Origin

The origins of filet mignon trace back to French culinary traditions. The term "filet mignon" itself is French, translating to "tender fillet" or "delicate fillet." It has been a staple in French haute cuisine for centuries, prized by chefs and diners alike for its exquisite flavor and texture.

C. Why Filet Mignon is Prized

Filet mignon's exceptional tenderness and mild flavor make it a favorite among steak connoisseurs. Unlike other cuts of beef, filet mignon contains very little fat marbling, which contributes to its tenderness but also means it has a milder taste compared to fattier cuts like ribeye or sirloin.

Its tenderness is attributed to the fact that it is cut from a muscle that receives minimal exercise, resulting in a more tender texture. Additionally, filet mignon is typically served in thick, uniform portions, allowing for even cooking and consistent tenderness throughout the steak.

Beyond its culinary attributes, filet mignon is often associated with elegance and indulgence, making it a popular choice for special occasions and fine dining experiences.

Chapter (1) Selecting and Preparing Filet Mignon

A. Choosing the Perfect Cut

When selecting filet mignon, it's essential to look for certain characteristics to ensure you get the best quality cut for your meal. Here are some tips for choosing the perfect filet mignon:

1. Marbling: While filet mignon is known for its leanness, a small amount of marbling can enhance flavor and tenderness. Look for a cut with fine marbling throughout the meat for optimal taste and texture.
2. Color: The meat should be bright red in color, indicating freshness. Avoid cuts that appear discolored or have a brownish hue.
3. Thickness: Opt for filet mignon steaks that are uniform in thickness to ensure even cooking. Thicker steaks are preferable as they allow for better control of the internal temperature during cooking.
4. Shape: Choose filet mignon steaks that are cylindrical in shape and free from irregularities or uneven thickness. This ensures consistent cooking and presentation.
5. Texture: The meat should feel firm to the touch but yield slightly when pressed. Avoid cuts that feel mushy or overly soft, as they may indicate poor quality or improper handling.

B. Handling and Storing Filet Mignon

Proper handling and storage are crucial for maintaining the quality and freshness of filet mignon. Follow these guidelines to ensure your meat stays in optimal condition:

1. Refrigeration: Upon purchasing filet mignon, refrigerate it

promptly to prevent bacterial growth. Store the meat in its original packaging or transfer it to an airtight container or sealed plastic bag.

2. Temperature: Keep filet mignon refrigerated at temperatures below 40°F (4°C) to slow bacterial growth and maintain freshness. Avoid storing it in the refrigerator door, as temperatures fluctuate more frequently in this area.

3. Storage Duration: Consume filet mignon within 2-3 days of purchase for the best quality. If you're not planning to use it immediately, consider freezing it for longer storage.

4. Freezing: To freeze filet mignon, wrap it tightly in plastic wrap or aluminum foil to prevent freezer burn. Place the wrapped steaks in a resealable freezer bag, removing as much air as possible before sealing. Label the bag with the date and store it in the freezer for up to 6 months.

C. Trimming and Preparing the Meat

Before cooking, it's essential to trim filet mignon to remove any excess fat or silver skin, which can affect the texture and flavor of the meat. Follow these steps to trim and prepare filet mignon:

1. Trimming: Using a sharp knife, carefully trim any visible fat or connective tissue from the surface of the steak. Pay close attention to the edges and seams where fat may be present.

2. Silver Skin Removal: Locate the thin, silvery membrane known as silver skin on the surface of the meat. Insert the tip of the knife under the silver skin and gently lift it away from the meat. Continue to trim away the silver skin, taking care not to remove too much meat in the process.

3. Seasoning: Once trimmed, season the filet mignon with your desired seasonings, such as salt, pepper, and herbs, to enhance flavor. Allow the meat to rest at room temperature for 15-30 minutes before cooking to ensure even cooking and optimal

flavor development.

By following these guidelines for selecting, handling, and preparing filet mignon, you can ensure a delicious and memorable dining experience every time.

Chapter (2) Essential Cooking Techniques

A. Searing

Searing is a high-heat cooking method used to brown the surface of meat quickly, creating a flavorful crust while sealing in juices. To sear filet mignon:

1. Preheat Pan: Heat a heavy-bottomed skillet or cast-iron pan over high heat until hot.
2. Season: Season the filet mignon with salt and pepper or your preferred seasonings.
3. Add Oil: Add a small amount of oil to the hot pan and swirl to coat the bottom evenly.
4. Sear: Carefully place the seasoned filet mignon in the hot pan and let it cook without moving for 2-3 minutes to develop a golden-brown crust.
5. Flip: Using tongs, flip the steak and sear the other side for an additional 2-3 minutes, or until desired doneness is reached.
6. Rest: Remove the steak from the pan and let it rest for a few minutes before serving to allow the juices to redistribute.

B. Grilling

Grilling is a popular method for cooking filet mignon, imparting a smoky flavor and beautiful grill marks. To grill filet mignon:

1. Preheat Grill: Preheat a gas or charcoal grill to medium-high heat (around 400°F to 450°F or 200°C to 230°C).
2. Season: Season the filet mignon with salt, pepper, and any desired seasonings.
3. Oil Grates: Brush the grill grates with oil to prevent sticking.
4. Grill: Place the seasoned filet mignon directly over the heat source and grill for 4-5 minutes on each side, or until grill marks

form and the desired level of doneness is achieved.

5. Rest: Remove the steak from the grill and let it rest for a few minutes before serving.

C. Roasting

Roasting filet mignon in the oven is a simple and foolproof method that yields tender and juicy results. To roast filet mignon:

1. Preheat Oven: Preheat the oven to 425°F (220°C).
2. Season: Season the filet mignon with salt, pepper, and any desired seasonings.
3. Sear (Optional): For extra flavor, sear the filet mignon in a hot skillet for 1-2 minutes per side before transferring it to the oven.
4. Roast: Place the seasoned filet mignon on a roasting rack set inside a roasting pan or directly on a baking sheet.
5. Cook: Roast the filet mignon in the preheated oven for 10-15 minutes, or until it reaches the desired level of doneness (use a meat thermometer for accuracy).
6. Rest: Remove the steak from the oven and let it rest for a few minutes before slicing and serving.

D. Pan-Searing

Pan-searing filet mignon on the stovetop is a quick and convenient method that yields delicious results. To pan-sear filet mignon:

1. Preheat Pan: Heat a heavy-bottomed skillet or cast-iron pan over medium-high heat until hot.
2. Season: Season the filet mignon with salt, pepper, and any desired seasonings.
3. Add Oil: Add a small amount of oil to the hot pan and swirl to coat the bottom evenly.
4. Sear: Carefully place the seasoned filet mignon in the hot pan and let it cook without moving for 3-4 minutes to develop a

golden-brown crust.

5. Flip: Using tongs, flip the steak and sear the other side for an additional 3-4 minutes, or until desired doneness is reached.

6. Rest: Remove the steak from the pan and let it rest for a few minutes before serving.

E. Sous Vide Method

Sous vide is a cooking technique that involves vacuum-sealing food in a bag and cooking it in a water bath at a precisely controlled temperature. To cook filet mignon using the sous vide method:

1. Preheat Water Bath: Fill a large pot or sous vide container with water and attach a sous vide precision cooker. Preheat the water to the desired cooking temperature (typically 130°F to 140°F or 54°C to 60°C for medium-rare).

2. Season: Season the filet mignon with salt, pepper, and any desired seasonings.

3. Vacuum Seal: Place the seasoned filet mignon in a vacuum-sealed bag or a resealable freezer bag, removing as much air as possible before sealing.

4. Cook: Submerge the sealed bag in the preheated water bath and cook the filet mignon for 1-2 hours, depending on the desired level of doneness.

5. Finish (Optional): After cooking sous vide, you can finish the filet mignon by searing it briefly on a hot skillet or grill to develop a caramelized crust.

6. Rest: Remove the steak from the bag and let it rest for a few minutes before serving.

By mastering these essential cooking techniques, you can prepare filet mignon to perfection and enjoy its exceptional flavor and tenderness.

Chapter (3) Mouthwatering Recipes

A. Classic Filet Mignon with Red Wine Reduction

Ingredients:

- 4 filet mignon steaks, about 1 1/2 inches thick
- Salt and pepper to taste
- 2 tablespoons olive oil
- 1 cup red wine
- 1/2 cup beef broth
- 2 tablespoons unsalted butter

Instructions:

1. Preheat your oven to 400°F (200°C).
2. Season the filet mignon steaks generously with salt and pepper.
3. Heat olive oil in an oven-proof skillet over medium-high heat.
4. Sear the filet mignon steaks for 3-4 minutes on each side until nicely browned.
5. Transfer the skillet to the preheated oven and roast for about 6-8 minutes for medium-rare, or until desired doneness is reached.
6. Remove the steaks from the skillet and let them rest on a plate while you prepare the sauce.
7. Place the skillet back on the stovetop over medium heat. Pour in the red wine and beef broth, scraping up any browned bits from the bottom of the pan.
8. Let the sauce simmer until it reduces by half, about 5-7 minutes.
9. Stir in the butter until melted and the sauce is smooth.
10. Serve the filet mignon with the red wine reduction sauce drizzled over the top.

B. Garlic Herb Butter Filet Mignon

Ingredients:

- 4 filet mignon steaks, about 1 1/2 inches thick
- Salt and pepper to taste
- 4 tablespoons unsalted butter, softened
- 2 cloves garlic, minced
- 2 tablespoons chopped fresh parsley
- 1 tablespoon chopped fresh thyme

Instructions:

1. Preheat your grill or grill pan to medium-high heat.
2. Season the filet mignon steaks with salt and pepper.
3. In a small bowl, mix together the softened butter, minced garlic, parsley, and thyme until well combined.
4. Spread a generous amount of the garlic herb butter over each filet mignon steak.
5. Grill the steaks for 4-5 minutes on each side, or until they reach the desired level of doneness.
6. Remove the steaks from the grill and let them rest for a few minutes before serving.

C. Bacon-Wrapped Filet Mignon
Ingredients:

- 4 filet mignon steaks, about 1 1/2 inches thick
- Salt and pepper to taste
- 8 slices bacon
- 2 tablespoons olive oil
- 2 tablespoons unsalted butter

Instructions:

1. Preheat your oven to 400°F (200°C).

2. Season the filet mignon steaks with salt and pepper.
3. Wrap each filet mignon steak with 2 slices of bacon, securing with toothpicks if necessary.
4. Heat olive oil and butter in an oven-proof skillet over medium-high heat.
5. Sear the bacon-wrapped filet mignon steaks for 3-4 minutes on each side until the bacon is crispy and the steaks are browned.
6. Transfer the skillet to the preheated oven and roast for about 6-8 minutes for medium-rare, or until desired doneness is reached.
7. Remove the steaks from the skillet and let them rest for a few minutes before serving.

D. Mushroom Stuffed Filet Mignon
Ingredients:

- 4 filet mignon steaks, about 1 1/2 inches thick
- Salt and pepper to taste
- 2 tablespoons olive oil
- 1 cup sliced mushrooms
- 2 cloves garlic, minced
- 1/4 cup chopped fresh parsley
- 1/4 cup grated Parmesan cheese

Instructions:

1. Preheat your oven to 400°F (200°C).
2. Season the filet mignon steaks with salt and pepper.
3. In a skillet, heat olive oil over medium heat. Add the sliced mushrooms and garlic, and sauté until the mushrooms are tender and browned.
4. Remove the skillet from heat and stir in the chopped parsley and grated Parmesan cheese.

5. Slice a pocket into each filet mignon steak, being careful not to cut all the way through.
6. Stuff each filet mignon with the mushroom mixture.
7. Heat olive oil in an oven-proof skillet over medium-high heat.
8. Sear the stuffed filet mignon steaks for 3-4 minutes on each side until nicely browned.
9. Transfer the skillet to the preheated oven and roast for about 6-8 minutes for medium-rare, or until desired doneness is reached.
10. Remove the steaks from the skillet and let them rest for a few minutes before serving.

E. Filet Mignon Oscar
Ingredients:

- 4 filet mignon steaks, about 1 1/2 inches thick
- Salt and pepper to taste
- 8 ounces cooked crab meat
- 4 asparagus spears, blanched
- Hollandaise sauce (store-bought or homemade)
- Chopped fresh parsley for garnish

Instructions:

1. Preheat your grill or grill pan to medium-high heat.
2. Season the filet mignon steaks with salt and pepper.
3. Grill the steaks for 4-5 minutes on each side, or until they reach the desired level of doneness.
4. Remove the steaks from the grill and let them rest for a few minutes.
5. Top each filet mignon steak with a portion of cooked crab meat and a blanched asparagus spear.
6. Drizzle hollandaise sauce over the top of each steak.

7. Garnish with chopped fresh parsley before serving.

F. Asian-inspired Soy Glazed Filet Mignon
Ingredients:

- 4 filet mignon steaks, about 1 1/2 inches thick
- Salt and pepper to taste
- 1/4 cup soy sauce
- 2 tablespoons honey
- 2 cloves garlic, minced
- 1 teaspoon grated fresh ginger
- 1 tablespoon sesame oil
- 2 green onions, thinly sliced (for garnish)
- Toasted sesame seeds (for garnish)

Instructions:

1. Season the filet mignon steaks with salt and pepper.
2. In a small bowl, whisk together soy sauce, honey, minced garlic, grated ginger, and sesame oil to make the glaze.
3. Place the filet mignon steaks in a shallow dish or resealable bag, and pour the glaze over them. Marinate for at least 30 minutes, or up to 2 hours in the refrigerator.
4. Preheat your grill or grill pan to medium-high heat.
5. Remove the steaks from the marinade and discard the excess marinade.
6. Grill the steaks for 4-5 minutes on each side, or until they reach the desired level of doneness.
7. Remove the steaks from the grill and let them rest for a few minutes before serving.
8. Garnish with sliced green onions and toasted sesame seeds before serving.

G. Filet Mignon with Béarnaise Sauce

Ingredients:

- 4 filet mignon steaks, about 1 1/2 inches thick
- Salt and pepper to taste
- 1 tablespoon olive oil
- 4 egg yolks
- 1 tablespoon white wine vinegar
- 1 tablespoon water
- 1/2 cup unsalted butter, melted
- 1 tablespoon chopped fresh tarragon
- Lemon juice to taste

Instructions:

1. Season the filet mignon steaks with salt and pepper.
2. Heat olive oil in a skillet over medium-high heat. Sear the steaks for 3-4 minutes on each side, or until they reach the desired level of doneness. Remove the steaks from the skillet and let them rest.
3. In a heatproof bowl, whisk together egg yolks, white wine vinegar, and water.
4. Place the bowl over a pot of simmering water (double boiler), making sure the bottom of the bowl doesn't touch the water. Whisk constantly until the mixture thickens and doubles in volume, about 3-4 minutes.
5. Slowly drizzle in the melted butter while whisking continuously until the sauce is smooth and thickened.
6. Stir in chopped fresh tarragon and lemon juice to taste. Season with salt and pepper if needed.
7. Serve the filet mignon steaks with the Béarnaise sauce spooned over the top.

H. Surf and Turf: Filet Mignon with Lobster Tail

Ingredients:

- 4 filet mignon steaks, about 1 1/2 inches thick
- Salt and pepper to taste
- 4 lobster tails
- Olive oil for brushing
- Lemon wedges for serving
- Melted butter for serving

Instructions:

1. Preheat your grill or grill pan to medium-high heat.
2. Season the filet mignon steaks with salt and pepper.
3. Brush the lobster tails with olive oil and season with salt and pepper.
4. Grill the filet mignon steaks for 4-5 minutes on each side, or until they reach the desired level of doneness.
5. Grill the lobster tails, shell side down, for 5-6 minutes, or until the shells are bright red and the meat is opaque.
6. Remove the steaks and lobster tails from the grill and let them rest for a few minutes.
7. Serve the filet mignon steaks with the grilled lobster tails, lemon wedges, and melted butter on the side.

I. Filet Mignon Sliders with Caramelized Onions

Ingredients:

- 1 lb ground beef chuck
- Salt and pepper to taste
- 8 slider buns
- 1 large onion, thinly sliced
- 2 tablespoons olive oil
- 2 tablespoons balsamic vinegar
- 1 tablespoon brown sugar

- Arugula leaves (optional)
- Sliced cheese (optional)

Instructions:

1. Divide the ground beef chuck into 8 equal portions and shape them into mini patties. Season with salt and pepper.
2. Heat olive oil in a skillet over medium-low heat. Add the sliced onions and cook, stirring occasionally, until they are caramelized and golden brown, about 20-25 minutes.
3. In a separate skillet or on a grill pan, cook the mini burger patties for 3-4 minutes on each side, or until they are cooked to your desired level of doneness.
4. In a small bowl, mix together balsamic vinegar and brown sugar. Add the mixture to the caramelized onions and cook for an additional 2-3 minutes, stirring frequently, until the onions are coated and slightly caramelized.
5. Toast the slider buns on the skillet or grill until lightly golden.
6. Assemble the sliders by placing a mini burger patty on the bottom half of each bun, followed by a spoonful of caramelized onions. Add arugula leaves and sliced cheese if desired. Top with the other half of the bun.
7. Serve the filet mignon sliders immediately.

J. Filet Mignon Salad with Balsamic Vinaigrette
Ingredients:

- 4 filet mignon steaks, about 1 1/2 inches thick
- Salt and pepper to taste
- 8 cups mixed salad greens
- 1 cup cherry tomatoes, halved
- 1/2 cup crumbled blue cheese
- 1/4 cup sliced almonds, toasted

- Balsamic vinaigrette (store-bought or homemade)

Instructions:

1. Season the filet mignon steaks with salt and pepper.
2. Heat olive oil in a skillet over medium-high heat. Sear the steaks for 3-4 minutes on each side, or until they reach the desired level of doneness. Remove the steaks from the skillet and let them rest.
3. In a large mixing bowl, combine the mixed salad greens, cherry tomatoes, crumbled blue cheese, and toasted sliced almonds.
4. Slice the filet mignon steaks thinly and arrange them on top of the salad.
5. Drizzle balsamic vinaigrette over the salad, toss gently to combine, and serve immediately.

Chapter (4) Sides and Accompaniments

A. Perfectly Paired Wines

Pairing the right wine with your filet mignon can enhance the dining experience. Here are some wine suggestions:

- Cabernet Sauvignon: This full-bodied red wine pairs well with the rich flavor of filet mignon, complementing its robust taste with notes of black currant, plum, and cedar.
- Merlot: With its soft tannins and fruity flavors of cherry and plum, Merlot is a versatile choice that pairs beautifully with filet mignon, especially if you prefer a smoother wine.
- Malbec: This Argentine red wine offers flavors of blackberry, dark cherry, and chocolate, making it an excellent match for the bold flavor of filet mignon.
- Syrah/Shiraz: Syrah/Shiraz wines are known for their intense flavors of blackberry, pepper, and spice, making them an ideal pairing for grilled or peppercorn-crusted filet mignon.
- Pinot Noir: For a lighter option, consider Pinot Noir with its silky texture and flavors of red berries, earth, and spice, which complement the tenderness of filet mignon without overpowering it.

Choose a wine based on your personal preference and the flavor profile of the dish you're serving with the filet mignon.

B. Decadent Sauces

Enhance the flavor of your filet mignon with these decadent sauce options:

- Peppercorn Sauce: Made with crushed black peppercorns, beef broth, cream, and a splash of brandy or cognac, this creamy sauce adds a bold, peppery flavor to your steak.
- Mushroom Sauce: A rich and earthy sauce made with sautéed mushrooms, shallots, garlic, beef broth, and a splash of red wine, finished with butter and fresh herbs like thyme or rosemary.
- Béarnaise Sauce: This classic French sauce combines clarified butter, egg yolks, white wine vinegar, and fresh tarragon to create a velvety smooth sauce with a delicate herbal flavor.
- Red Wine Reduction: A simple yet elegant sauce made by reducing red wine with shallots, garlic, and beef broth until thickened and flavorful, perfect for drizzling over your steak.
- Blue Cheese Sauce: A creamy sauce made with blue cheese, cream, butter, and a splash of white wine or brandy, offering a tangy and savory complement to the richness of filet mignon.

Choose a sauce that complements the flavors of your filet mignon and suits your personal taste preferences.

C. Potato Dishes

Accompany your filet mignon with one of these delicious potato dishes:

- Creamy Mashed Potatoes: Fluffy mashed potatoes made with butter, cream, and seasoning, providing a creamy and comforting side dish.
- Roasted Potatoes: Bite-sized potatoes roasted with olive oil, garlic, and herbs until crispy on the outside and tender on the inside, offering a flavorful contrast to the steak.
- Potato Gratin: Thinly sliced potatoes layered with cream, garlic,

and cheese, baked until golden and bubbling, creating a decadent and indulgent side dish.

- Loaded Baked Potatoes: Baked potatoes topped with butter, sour cream, crispy bacon, chives, and shredded cheese, offering a hearty and satisfying accompaniment to your steak.
- Potato Dauphinoise: Thinly sliced potatoes baked in a creamy garlic-infused sauce, resulting in a rich and flavorful potato casserole.

Choose a potato dish that complements the richness of the filet mignon and adds texture and flavor to your meal.

D. Vegetable Medleys

Add vibrant colors and flavors to your meal with these vegetable medley options:

- Roasted Vegetables: A mix of seasonal vegetables such as carrots, bell peppers, zucchini, and onions tossed with olive oil, garlic, and herbs, roasted until caramelized and tender.
- Grilled Asparagus: Fresh asparagus spears seasoned with olive oil, salt, and pepper, grilled until charred and tender, offering a simple yet elegant side dish.
- Sautéed Green Beans: Crisp-tender green beans sautéed with garlic, shallots, and almonds, providing a flavorful and nutritious accompaniment to your steak.
- Steamed Broccoli with Lemon Butter: Steamed broccoli florets tossed with melted butter, lemon juice, and zest, seasoned with salt and pepper, offering a bright and refreshing side dish.
- Glazed Carrots: Tender baby carrots simmered in a honey and butter glaze until caramelized and sweet, providing a delightful contrast to the savory flavors of the steak.

Choose a vegetable medley that complements the flavors of your filet mignon and adds freshness and color to your plate.

E. Salad Complements

Balance the richness of your filet mignon with a refreshing salad:

- Classic Caesar Salad: Crisp romaine lettuce tossed with Caesar dressing, Parmesan cheese, and garlic croutons, offering a tangy and creamy accompaniment to your steak.
- Caprese Salad: Slices of ripe tomatoes, fresh mozzarella cheese, and basil leaves drizzled with balsamic glaze and olive oil, providing a light and flavorful side dish.
- Arugula and Parmesan Salad: Peppery arugula tossed with shaved Parmesan cheese, lemon vinaigrette, and toasted pine nuts, offering a bright and refreshing complement to your meal.
- Mixed Greens Salad: A mix of tender salad greens such as spinach, mesclun, and watercress tossed with a light vinaigrette, providing a crisp and refreshing side dish.
- Greek Salad: Chopped cucumbers, tomatoes, red onions, Kalamata olives, and feta cheese tossed with a Greek vinaigrette, offering a vibrant and flavorful accompaniment to your steak.

Choose a salad that complements the flavors of your filet mignon and adds freshness and texture to your meal.

Chapter (5) Tips and Techniques for Perfection

A. Achieving the Perfect Temperature

- Use a Meat Thermometer: Invest in a reliable meat thermometer to ensure accuracy when checking the internal temperature of your filet mignon. Aim for the following temperature ranges for desired doneness:

✓ Rare: 120-125°F (49-52°C)
✓ Medium Rare: 130-135°F (54-57°C)
✓ Medium: 140-145°F (60-63°C)
✓ Medium Well: 150-155°F (66-68°C)
✓ Well Done: 160°F (71°C) and above

- Allow for Carryover Cooking: Keep in mind that the internal temperature of the steak will continue to rise by a few degrees after removing it from the heat source. Therefore, it's advisable to remove the steak from the heat when it's a few degrees below your desired doneness.

B. Resting and Slicing

1. Resting Time: After cooking, allow your filet mignon to rest for at least 5-10 minutes before slicing or serving. Resting allows the juices to redistribute throughout the meat, resulting in a juicier and more flavorful steak.
2. Slicing Technique: When slicing your filet mignon, use a sharp knife and cut against the grain for maximum tenderness. Aim for uniform slices to ensure even distribution of flavor and texture.

C. Troubleshooting Common Issues

1. Overcooking: To prevent overcooking, monitor the internal temperature of the filet mignon closely and remove it from the heat source promptly when it reaches your desired level of doneness.

2. Dryness: Avoid overcooking or using high heat for too long, as this can result in a dry and tough steak. Consider using a marinade, sauce, or basting with butter to add moisture and flavor to the meat.

3. Uneven Cooking: Ensure that your filet mignon steaks are of uniform thickness to promote even cooking. If necessary, use a meat mallet to gently pound thicker parts of the steak to an even thickness.

D. Presentation and Plating Tips

1. Plate Presentation: Arrange your filet mignon and accompanying sides on a clean, well-presented plate. Consider using garnishes such as fresh herbs, lemon wedges, or edible flowers to add color and visual appeal to the dish.

2. Sauce Drizzling: When serving with sauces, drizzle them elegantly over the steak or alongside for dipping. Use a spoon or squeeze bottle for precise and attractive presentation.

3. Garnish and Texture: Add texture and contrast to your dish by incorporating garnishes such as crispy fried onions, toasted nuts, or microgreens. These elements not only enhance the visual appeal but also provide additional flavor and texture to each bite.

Chapter (6) Beyond the Basics

A. Advanced Cooking Techniques

1. Sous Vide Cooking: Utilize sous vide cooking for precise temperature control and consistent results. Vacuum-seal seasoned filet mignon and cook it in a water bath at the desired temperature for a set amount of time, then finish with a quick sear for flavor and texture.

2. Reverse Searing: Reverse searing involves cooking the filet mignon in a low-temperature oven or sous vide cooker until it reaches the desired internal temperature, then finishing with a high-heat sear to develop a crust. This method ensures a perfectly cooked steak with a tender interior and caramelized exterior.

3. Smoking: Experiment with smoking filet mignon to infuse it with rich, smoky flavor. Use wood chips or chunks in a smoker or grill to impart a unique taste profile to the steak, complementing its natural beefiness.

B. Fusion and International Flavors

1. Mediterranean: Incorporate Mediterranean flavors by seasoning filet mignon with a blend of olive oil, garlic, lemon zest, and oregano before grilling or roasting. Serve with a side of tzatziki sauce and a Greek salad for a refreshing and flavorful meal.

2. Asian: Infuse filet mignon with Asian-inspired flavors by marinating it in a mixture of soy sauce, ginger, garlic, and sesame oil before grilling or pan-searing. Serve with steamed rice and stir-fried vegetables for a delicious fusion dish.

3. Latin American: Create a Latin American-inspired dish by

seasoning filet mignon with a blend of cumin, chili powder, and lime juice before grilling or broiling. Serve with black beans, rice, and fresh salsa for a vibrant and satisfying meal.

C. Filet Mignon in Fine Dining

1. Beef Wellington: Elevate filet mignon to gourmet status by preparing it as Beef Wellington—a classic dish consisting of filet mignon coated with pâté and duxelles (a mixture of finely chopped mushrooms, shallots, and herbs), wrapped in puff pastry, and baked until golden brown. Serve with a rich red wine sauce for a luxurious dining experience.

2. Chateaubriand: Serve filet mignon as Chateaubriand—a center-cut portion of the beef tenderloin that is roasted and served with Béarnaise sauce. This elegant dish is perfect for special occasions and showcases the exquisite flavor and tenderness of the filet mignon.

3. Steak Diane: Prepare filet mignon in the classic Steak Diane style—pan-seared and served with a rich sauce made from shallots, mushrooms, Dijon mustard, Worcestershire sauce, and brandy. This sophisticated dish is flambeed tableside for a dramatic presentation and unforgettable flavor.

Chapter (7) Sides and Accompaniments (continued)

A. Wine Pairing Guide

Pairing the right wine with your filet mignon can elevate the dining experience. Here's a guide to wine pairing:

1. Cabernet Sauvignon: Known for its bold flavors of black currant and cedar, Cabernet Sauvignon is a classic pairing for filet mignon, especially when prepared with rich sauces or seasonings.
2. Merlot: With its softer tannins and fruity notes of plum and cherry, Merlot complements the tender texture of filet mignon, making it an excellent choice for those who prefer a smoother wine.
3. Pinot Noir: Offering flavors of red berries and earthy undertones, Pinot Noir pairs well with filet mignon prepared with lighter sauces or seasonings, enhancing the natural flavors of the meat.
4. Malbec: This Argentine red wine boasts flavors of blackberry and spice, making it a great match for grilled or spicier preparations of filet mignon.
5. Syrah/Shiraz: With its bold flavors of blackberry and pepper, Syrah/Shiraz is ideal for pairing with peppercorn-crusted or grilled filet mignon, adding depth and complexity to the dish.

Consider the flavors and seasonings used in your filet mignon preparation when selecting the perfect wine pairing.

B. Homemade Compound Butters

Enhance the flavor of your filet mignon with homemade compound butters:

1. Garlic Herb Butter: Mix softened butter with minced garlic, chopped fresh herbs such as parsley, thyme, and rosemary, and a pinch of salt and pepper. Roll into a log, wrap in plastic wrap, and chill until firm. Slice and place a pat of garlic herb butter on top of each cooked steak before serving.
2. Truffle Butter: Combine softened butter with finely grated truffle or truffle oil, minced chives, and a pinch of salt. Roll into a log, wrap in plastic wrap, and chill until firm. Slice and serve with filet mignon for a luxurious touch.
3. Blue Cheese Butter: Mash together softened butter with crumbled blue cheese, minced shallots, and a dash of Worcestershire sauce. Form into a log, wrap in plastic wrap, and chill until firm. Slice and place a dollop on top of each cooked steak for a decadent finish.

Experiment with different flavor combinations to create custom compound butters that complement your filet mignon.

C. Grilled Vegetable Platters

Serve grilled vegetable platters alongside your filet mignon for a flavorful and nutritious accompaniment:

1. Grilled Asparagus: Toss asparagus spears with olive oil, salt, and pepper, then grill until tender and lightly charred. Serve with a squeeze of lemon juice for brightness.
2. Grilled Zucchini and Squash: Slice zucchini and yellow squash into thick rounds, brush with olive oil, and season with salt, pepper, and Italian herbs. Grill until tender and caramelized.
3. Grilled Bell Peppers: Cut bell peppers into large strips, toss with olive oil, salt, and pepper, then grill until softened and charred.

Serve with a drizzle of balsamic glaze for added flavor.

Arrange the grilled vegetables on a platter and garnish with fresh herbs for a vibrant and visually appealing side dish.

D. Creamy Mashed Potatoes Variations

Elevate classic mashed potatoes with these variations:

1. Garlic Parmesan Mashed Potatoes: Add roasted garlic cloves and grated Parmesan cheese to mashed potatoes for a savory and indulgent twist.
2. Loaded Mashed Potatoes: Mix in cooked and crumbled bacon, shredded cheddar cheese, and chopped chives to mashed potatoes for a decadent and flavorful side dish.
3. Horseradish Mashed Potatoes: Stir prepared horseradish into mashed potatoes for a spicy kick and extra depth of flavor that pairs well with steak.

Experiment with different ingredients and seasonings to create mashed potato variations that complement your filet mignon.

E. Seasonal Salad Inspirations

Incorporate seasonal ingredients into salads to accompany your filet mignon:

1. Summer Berry Salad: Combine mixed greens with fresh strawberries, blueberries, raspberries, and toasted almonds. Drizzle with balsamic vinaigrette for a sweet and tangy flavor profile.
2. Autumn Harvest Salad: Toss mixed greens with roasted butternut squash, dried cranberries, toasted pecans, and crumbled goat cheese. Dress with maple balsamic vinaigrette for a taste of fall.

3. Winter Citrus Salad: Mix arugula with segments of grapefruit and orange, pomegranate seeds, thinly sliced red onion, and feta cheese. Finish with a citrus vinaigrette for a refreshing and vibrant salad.

4. Spring Vegetable Salad: Combine baby spinach with blanched asparagus, English peas, shaved radishes, and crumbled feta cheese. Drizzle with lemon herb vinaigrette for a light and fresh salad option.

Tailor your salad selections to the season to highlight the freshest ingredients and complement the flavors of your filet mignon.

Chapter (8) Tips and Techniques for Perfection (continued)

A. Marinating and Seasoning Tips

1. Use a Dry Rub: Apply a dry rub of herbs, spices, and seasonings to your filet mignon before cooking to add flavor and enhance the crust. Allow the rub to sit on the steak for at least 30 minutes, or overnight in the refrigerator, to penetrate the meat.
2. Marinate for Flavor: Marinate filet mignon in a mixture of oil, acid (such as vinegar or citrus juice), and seasonings for added flavor and tenderness. Keep in mind that filet mignon is already tender, so marinate for a shorter period (1-2 hours) to avoid overpowering the natural flavor of the meat.

B. Proper Knife Skills for Trimming and Slicing

1. Trimming: Use a sharp knife to carefully trim any excess fat or silver skin from the filet mignon before cooking. Removing these unwanted portions ensures even cooking and a more appealing presentation.
2. Slicing: When slicing cooked filet mignon, use a sharp carving knife or chef's knife and cut against the grain for maximum tenderness. Aim for uniform slices to ensure consistent texture and flavor throughout.

C. Utilizing Meat Thermometers

1. Instant-Read Thermometer: Invest in a quality instant-read meat thermometer to accurately gauge the internal temperature of your filet mignon. Insert the thermometer into the thickest part of the steak for the most accurate reading.
2. Digital Probe Thermometer: Consider using a digital probe

thermometer with a temperature alarm feature for hands-free monitoring of the steak's internal temperature. Set the desired temperature and receive an alert when the steak reaches the perfect level of doneness.

D. Managing Cooking Times for Different Thicknesses

1. Adjust Cooking Time: Thicker filet mignon steaks will require longer cooking times to reach the desired level of doneness compared to thinner cuts. Adjust your cooking time accordingly, keeping in mind that thicker steaks will retain heat and continue cooking even after being removed from the heat source.

2. Use a Timer: Keep track of cooking times using a kitchen timer or smartphone app to ensure that your filet mignon is cooked to perfection. Follow recommended cooking times based on the thickness of the steak and your desired level of doneness.

E. Adjusting Flavors with Seasonings and Rubs

1. Experiment with Seasonings: Customize the flavor of your filet mignon by experimenting with different herbs, spices, and seasonings. Common options include garlic powder, onion powder, smoked paprika, cumin, and chili powder. Adjust the amounts to suit your taste preferences.

2. Balance Flavors: When creating rubs or seasoning blends for filet mignon, strive for a balance of savory, sweet, acidic, and spicy elements. Taste as you go and adjust the seasoning accordingly to achieve the perfect flavor profile.

Chapter (9) Special Occasion Recipes

A. Filet Mignon Wellington
Ingredients:

- 4 filet mignon steaks, about 1 1/2 inches thick
- Salt and pepper to taste
- 1 tablespoon olive oil
- 8 slices prosciutto
- 2 tablespoons Dijon mustard
- 1 sheet puff pastry, thawed
- 1 egg, beaten (for egg wash)

Mushroom Duxelles:

- 2 cups finely chopped mushrooms
- 2 shallots, finely chopped
- 2 cloves garlic, minced
- 2 tablespoons butter
- Salt and pepper to taste
- 1/4 cup dry white wine
- Béarnaise sauce (optional, for serving)

Instructions:

1. Season the filet mignon steaks with salt and pepper.
2. In a skillet, heat olive oil over medium-high heat. Sear the steaks for 2 minutes on each side. Remove from heat and let cool.
3. Prepare the mushroom duxelles: In the same skillet, melt butter over medium heat. Add shallots and garlic, sauté until softened. Add chopped mushrooms, salt, and pepper. Cook until the mushrooms release their moisture and become golden brown. Deglaze the skillet with white wine, scraping up any browned

bits from the bottom. Let cool.

4. Roll out the puff pastry on a lightly floured surface. Spread Dijon mustard on each slice of prosciutto. Place a layer of prosciutto over the pastry, then spread the mushroom duxelles on top.
5. Place the seared filet mignon steaks on top of the mushroom duxelles. Wrap the pastry around the steaks, sealing the edges tightly.
6. Brush the pastry with beaten egg for an egg wash.
7. Preheat the oven to 400°F (200°C). Place the wrapped filet mignon on a baking sheet lined with parchment paper.
8. Bake for 25-30 minutes or until the pastry is golden brown and the steaks reach the desired level of doneness.
9. Let the Filet Mignon Wellington rest for a few minutes before slicing. Serve with Béarnaise sauce if desired.

B. Filet Mignon with Truffle Butter

Ingredients:

- 4 filet mignon steaks, about 1 1/2 inches thick
- Salt and pepper to taste
- 2 tablespoons truffle butter
- Fresh parsley, chopped (for garnish)

Instructions:

1. Season the filet mignon steaks with salt and pepper.
2. Heat a skillet over medium-high heat. Add the steaks and cook for 4-5 minutes on each side for medium-rare, or until they reach the desired level of doneness.
3. Remove the steaks from the skillet and let them rest for a few minutes.
4. Place a tablespoon of truffle butter on top of each steak while

still warm, allowing it to melt slightly.

5. Garnish with chopped parsley before serving.

C. Filet Mignon with Foie Gras
Ingredients:

- 4 filet mignon steaks, about 1 1/2 inches thick
- Salt and pepper to taste
- 4 slices foie gras
- 2 tablespoons butter
- 2 tablespoons brandy
- 1/2 cup beef broth
- Fresh thyme leaves (for garnish)

Instructions:

1. Season the filet mignon steaks with salt and pepper.
2. In a skillet over medium-high heat, melt butter. Add the steaks and cook for 4-5 minutes on each side for medium-rare, or until they reach the desired level of doneness.
3. Remove the steaks from the skillet and let them rest for a few minutes.
4. In the same skillet, add brandy and deglaze the pan. Add beef broth and bring to a simmer, scraping up any browned bits.
5. Return the steaks to the skillet. Top each steak with a slice of foie gras. Cover the skillet and let it sit for 1-2 minutes, allowing the foie gras to melt slightly.
6. Transfer the steaks to serving plates, spooning the sauce over the top. Garnish with fresh thyme leaves before serving.

D. Filet Mignon Tartare
Ingredients:

- 1 lb filet mignon, finely chopped

- 2 tablespoons capers, drained and chopped
- 2 tablespoons red onion, finely chopped
- 2 tablespoons fresh parsley, chopped
- 2 tablespoons Dijon mustard
- 1 tablespoon Worcestershire sauce
- 1 tablespoon olive oil
- Salt and pepper to taste
- 4 egg yolks (for serving)
- Toasted baguette slices (for serving)

Instructions:

1. In a mixing bowl, combine chopped filet mignon, capers, red onion, parsley, Dijon mustard, Worcestershire sauce, and olive oil. Season with salt and pepper to taste.
2. Mix well until all ingredients are evenly combined.
3. Divide the filet mignon mixture into 4 portions and shape each portion into a mound on individual serving plates.
4. Create a small well in the center of each mound and place an egg yolk in each well.
5. Serve the filet mignon tartare with toasted baguette slices for spreading.

E. Filet Mignon Carpaccio
Ingredients:

- 1 lb filet mignon, thinly sliced
- 2 cups arugula
- 1/4 cup shaved Parmesan cheese
- 2 tablespoons extra virgin olive oil
- 1 tablespoon lemon juice
- Salt and pepper to taste

Instructions:

1. Arrange the thinly sliced filet mignon on a serving platter in a single layer.
2. In a small bowl, whisk together extra virgin olive oil, lemon juice, salt, and pepper to make a dressing.
3. Drizzle the dressing over the sliced filet mignon.
4. Top the filet mignon with arugula and shaved Parmesan cheese.
5. Serve immediately as a light and elegant appetizer.

Chapter (10) Healthier Alternatives and Dietary Considerations

A. Lean Cooking Methods for Filet Mignon

1. Grilling: Grill filet mignon over high heat for a shorter cooking time, which helps to preserve its natural juices without the need for additional fats.
2. Broiling: Broil filet mignon in the oven on a rack positioned close to the heating element. This method allows excess fat to drip away from the meat while it cooks, resulting in a leaner dish.
3. Pan-Searing: Sear filet mignon in a hot skillet with a small amount of oil or cooking spray. Searing quickly seals in juices and adds flavor without excessive added fats.

B. Filet Mignon in Low-Carb Diets

1. Grilled Filet Mignon with Vegetables: Serve grilled filet mignon alongside low-carb vegetables such as asparagus, zucchini, and bell peppers for a satisfying and nutritious meal.
2. Filet Mignon Salad: Thinly slice grilled or seared filet mignon and serve it atop a bed of mixed greens with sliced avocado, cherry tomatoes, and a drizzle of olive oil and balsamic vinegar.
3. Stuffed Portobello Mushrooms: Fill portobello mushroom caps with seasoned ground beef or chopped filet mignon, top with cheese, and bake until bubbly and golden for a low-carb alternative to traditional steak dishes.

C. Gluten-Free Filet Mignon Recipes

1. Grilled Filet Mignon with Chimichurri Sauce: Marinate filet mignon steaks in a gluten-free chimichurri sauce made with

fresh herbs, garlic, olive oil, and vinegar before grilling for a flavorful and gluten-free dish.

2. Filet Mignon Skewers: Thread cubes of filet mignon onto skewers with vegetables such as cherry tomatoes, bell peppers, and onions. Grill or broil until the steak is cooked to your desired doneness for a gluten-free and colorful meal.

3. Filet Mignon Lettuce Wraps: Serve thinly sliced filet mignon wrapped in butter lettuce leaves with gluten-free dipping sauces such as tamari or homemade aioli for a light and gluten-free alternative to traditional steak wraps.

D. Filet Mignon for Paleo and Keto Diets

1. Bacon-Wrapped Filet Mignon: Wrap filet mignon steaks with sugar-free bacon slices before grilling or broiling for a flavorful and indulgent dish that is suitable for paleo and keto diets.

2. Filet Mignon Stir-Fry: Thinly slice filet mignon and stir-fry with low-carb vegetables such as broccoli, bell peppers, and snap peas in a paleo-friendly sauce made with coconut aminos, garlic, and ginger.

3. Cauliflower Mash with Filet Mignon: Serve filet mignon alongside mashed cauliflower seasoned with ghee, garlic, and herbs for a satisfying and low-carb alternative to traditional mashed potatoes.

E. Vegetarian and Vegan Options with Filet Mignon Substitute

1. Portobello Mushroom Steaks: Grill or roast large portobello mushroom caps marinated in balsamic vinegar, olive oil, and herbs as a meaty and satisfying alternative to filet mignon for vegetarians and vegans.

2. Eggplant Steaks: Slice thick rounds of eggplant and grill or roast until tender, then serve with your favorite sauce or

seasoning for a hearty and plant-based alternative to traditional steak dishes.

3. Seitan or Tempeh Steak: Marinate and grill seitan or tempeh steaks for a protein-rich and vegan-friendly alternative to filet mignon. Serve with roasted vegetables or a side salad for a complete meal.

Chapter (11) Family-Friendly Filet Mignon

A. Kid-Friendly Filet Mignon Recipes

1. Mini Filet Mignon Sliders: Grill or pan-sear mini filet mignon patties and serve them on slider buns with lettuce, tomato, and a dollop of ketchup or barbecue sauce for a fun and kid-friendly meal.

2. Filet Mignon Skewers: Cut filet mignon into bite-sized cubes and thread them onto skewers with colorful vegetables such as cherry tomatoes, bell peppers, and mushrooms. Grill or broil until cooked to perfection for a tasty and easy-to-eat dish.

3. Filet Mignon Quesadillas: Fill flour tortillas with shredded cheese and thinly sliced cooked filet mignon. Fold the tortillas in half and cook them on a skillet until the cheese is melted and the tortillas are crispy. Serve with salsa and guacamole for dipping.

B. Quick and Easy Filet Mignon Meals for Busy Weeknights

1. Filet Mignon Stir-Fry: Quickly sear thinly sliced filet mignon with garlic, ginger, and your favorite stir-fry vegetables in a hot skillet or wok. Add a splash of soy sauce or teriyaki sauce for flavor, and serve over cooked rice or noodles for a satisfying meal in minutes.

2. Filet Mignon Salad Wraps: Slice leftover filet mignon thinly and wrap it in large lettuce leaves with shredded carrots, cucumber slices, and a drizzle of your favorite dressing for a light and refreshing meal that comes together in no time.

3. Filet Mignon Tacos: Shred cooked filet mignon and serve it in taco shells or tortillas with your choice of toppings such as

shredded lettuce, diced tomatoes, avocado slices, and salsa for a quick and customizable dinner option.

C. Cooking with Filet Mignon Leftovers

1. Filet Mignon Hash: Chop leftover filet mignon into bite-sized pieces and sauté it with diced potatoes, onions, and bell peppers until crispy and golden brown. Serve topped with fried eggs for a hearty breakfast or brunch option.

2. Filet Mignon Fried Rice: Dice leftover filet mignon and stir-fry it with cooked rice, scrambled eggs, peas, carrots, and soy sauce for a flavorful and satisfying fried rice dish that's perfect for using up leftovers.

3. Filet Mignon Sandwiches: Thinly slice leftover filet mignon and layer it on crusty bread with your favorite sandwich toppings such as lettuce, tomato, and mayonnaise for a delicious and convenient lunch option.

Chapter (12) Holiday and Celebration Menus

A. Filet Mignon Feast for Christmas
   Appetizer:

- Bacon-Wrapped Scallops: Succulent scallops wrapped in crispy bacon, served with a tangy citrus aioli dipping sauce.

Main Course:

- Filet Mignon Wellington: Tender filet mignon wrapped in prosciutto and mushroom duxelles, encased in flaky puff pastry and baked to perfection.
- Roasted Garlic Mashed Potatoes: Creamy mashed potatoes infused with roasted garlic, butter, and fresh herbs.
- Green Bean Almondine: Tender green beans sautéed with garlic, lemon zest, and toasted almonds.
- Red Wine Reduction Sauce: A rich and savory sauce made from red wine, beef broth, and aromatics, drizzled over the filet mignon Wellington.

Dessert:

- Chocolate Lava Cake: Decadent chocolate cakes with a molten center, served warm with a scoop of vanilla ice cream and a dusting of powdered sugar.

B. Romantic Valentine's Day Filet Mignon Dinner
   Appetizer:

- Caprese Salad: Slices of ripe tomatoes and fresh mozzarella, layered with basil leaves and drizzled with balsamic glaze.

Main Course:

- Garlic Herb Butter Filet Mignon: Juicy filet mignon steaks seared to perfection and topped with a pat of garlic herb butter.
- Lobster Tail: Succulent lobster tails broiled with garlic butter and lemon, served alongside the filet mignon.
- Asparagus Bundles: Tender asparagus spears wrapped in prosciutto and roasted until crispy.
- Truffle Parmesan Risotto: Creamy risotto infused with truffle oil and finished with grated Parmesan cheese.

Dessert:

- Raspberry Chocolate Tart: Buttery tart crust filled with rich chocolate ganache and topped with fresh raspberries.

C. Easter Sunday Filet Mignon Brunch
Appetizer:

- Deviled Eggs: Hard-boiled eggs filled with a creamy mixture of egg yolks, mayonnaise, mustard, and spices, garnished with paprika and fresh chives.

Main Course:

- Filet Mignon Benedict: Grilled filet mignon medallions served on toasted English muffins with poached eggs and hollandaise sauce.
- Roasted Potato Hash: Crispy roasted potatoes tossed with bell peppers, onions, and herbs, served alongside the Filet Mignon Benedict.

- Grilled Asparagus with Lemon: Fresh asparagus spears grilled until tender and lightly charred, finished with a squeeze of lemon juice.

Dessert:

- Lemon Blueberry Scones: Tender scones studded with juicy blueberries and brightened with fresh lemon zest, served with clotted cream and lemon curd.

Chapter (13) Filet Mignon Appetizers and Small Bites

A. Filet Mignon Skewers with Chimichurri Sauce
  Ingredients:

- 1 lb filet mignon, cut into 1-inch cubes
- Salt and pepper, to taste
- Wooden skewers, soaked in water for 30 minutes

Chimichurri Sauce:

- 1 cup fresh parsley, finely chopped
- 1/4 cup fresh cilantro, finely chopped
- 3 cloves garlic, minced
- 1/4 cup red wine vinegar
- 1/2 cup extra virgin olive oil
- 1/2 teaspoon red pepper flakes
- Salt and pepper, to taste

Instructions:

1. Season the filet mignon cubes with salt and pepper.
2. Thread the seasoned filet mignon cubes onto the soaked wooden skewers.
3. Preheat a grill or grill pan over medium-high heat. Grill the skewers for 2-3 minutes per side, or until desired doneness is reached.
4. Meanwhile, prepare the chimichurri sauce. In a small bowl, combine the parsley, cilantro, garlic, red wine vinegar, olive oil, red pepper flakes, salt, and pepper. Mix well.
5. Serve the grilled filet mignon skewers with chimichurri sauce on the side for dipping.

B. Filet Mignon Crostini with Gorgonzola and Caramelized Onions

Ingredients:

- Baguette, thinly sliced
- Olive oil
- 1 lb filet mignon, thinly sliced
- Salt and pepper, to taste
- Gorgonzola cheese, crumbled

Caramelized onions:

- 2 large onions, thinly sliced
- 2 tablespoons butter
- 1 tablespoon olive oil
- Salt and pepper, to taste

Instructions:

1. Preheat the oven to 375°F (190°C).
2. Place the baguette slices on a baking sheet and brush each slice lightly with olive oil. Bake for 8-10 minutes, or until the slices are lightly toasted. Remove from the oven and set aside.
3. Season the thinly sliced filet mignon with salt and pepper.
4. Heat a skillet over medium-high heat. Add a drizzle of olive oil and sear the filet mignon slices for 1-2 minutes on each side, or until browned. Remove from the skillet and set aside.
5. In the same skillet, melt butter and olive oil over medium heat. Add the thinly sliced onions and cook, stirring occasionally, until caramelized and golden brown, about 20-25 minutes. Season with salt and pepper.
6. To assemble the crostini, spread a layer of caramelized onions on each toasted baguette slice. Top with a slice of seared filet mignon and crumbled Gorgonzola cheese.

7. Return the assembled crostini to the oven and bake for an additional 5 minutes, or until the cheese is melted and bubbly.
8. Serve the filet mignon crostini warm.

C. Filet Mignon Sliders with Horseradish Cream

Ingredients:

- Slider buns
- 1 lb filet mignon, thinly sliced
- Salt and pepper, to taste
- Olive oil

Horseradish Cream:

- 1/2 cup sour cream
- 2 tablespoons prepared horseradish
- 1 tablespoon Dijon mustard
- 1 tablespoon fresh lemon juice
- Salt and pepper, to taste

Instructions:

1. Preheat a grill or grill pan over medium-high heat.
2. Season the thinly sliced filet mignon with salt and pepper.
3. Drizzle olive oil over the seasoned filet mignon slices.
4. Grill the filet mignon slices for 1-2 minutes per side, or until cooked to your desired level of doneness. Remove from the grill and let rest.
5. Meanwhile, prepare the horseradish cream. In a small bowl, combine the sour cream, prepared horseradish, Dijon mustard, fresh lemon juice, salt, and pepper. Mix well.
6. To assemble the sliders, spread a dollop of horseradish cream on the bottom half of each slider bun. Top with a slice of grilled filet mignon and the top half of the bun.

7. Secure each slider with a toothpick and serve.

Chapter (14) Global Filet Mignon Variations

A. Japanese Wagyu Filet Mignon Recipes
Wagyu Filet Mignon Tataki
Ingredients:

- 1 lb Wagyu filet mignon, thinly sliced
- 2 tablespoons soy sauce
- 1 tablespoon mirin (Japanese sweet rice wine)
- 1 tablespoon sake (Japanese rice wine)
- 1 teaspoon sesame oil
- 2 cloves garlic, minced
- 1-inch piece ginger, grated
- 2 green onions, thinly sliced
- Toasted sesame seeds, for garnish
- Shichimi togarashi (Japanese seven-spice blend), for garnish
- Fresh cilantro leaves, for garnish

Instructions:

1. In a bowl, combine soy sauce, mirin, sake, sesame oil, minced garlic, and grated ginger to make the marinade.
2. Marinate the thinly sliced Wagyu filet mignon in the marinade for 15-30 minutes.
3. Heat a skillet over high heat. Sear the marinated filet mignon slices for about 30 seconds on each side, or until lightly browned but still rare in the center.
4. Remove the seared filet mignon slices from the skillet and arrange them on a serving platter.
5. Garnish with sliced green onions, toasted sesame seeds, shichimi togarashi, and fresh cilantro leaves.

6. Serve immediately as an appetizer or light main course.

B. Brazilian Churrasco Style Filet Mignon
Filet Mignon Wrapped in Bacon (Filet Mignon Enrolado com Bacon)
Ingredients:

- 4 filet mignon steaks, about 1 1/2 inches thick
- Salt and pepper, to taste
- 8 slices bacon
- Wooden skewers, soaked in water for 30 minutes

Instructions:

1. Season the filet mignon steaks with salt and pepper.
2. Wrap each filet mignon steak with 2 slices of bacon, securing them in place with wooden skewers.
3. Preheat a grill to medium-high heat. Grill the bacon-wrapped filet mignon for 4-5 minutes on each side, or until the bacon is crispy and the steak is cooked to your desired level of doneness.
4. Remove the skewers before serving.
5. Serve the filet mignon wrapped in bacon hot off the grill, accompanied by traditional Brazilian side dishes such as farofa, rice, and Brazilian-style vinaigrette.

C. French Filet Mignon Escalopes
Filet Mignon Escalopes with Mushroom Cream Sauce (Escalopes de Filet Mignon com Molho de Cogumelos)
Ingredients:

- 4 filet mignon steaks, pounded to 1/4-inch thickness
- Salt and pepper, to taste
- 2 tablespoons olive oil
- 2 tablespoons butter
- 8 oz mushrooms, sliced
- 2 cloves garlic, minced
- 1/4 cup white wine
- 1 cup heavy cream
- 2 tablespoons fresh parsley, chopped

Instructions:

1. Season the pounded filet mignon steaks with salt and pepper on both sides.
2. Heat olive oil and butter in a skillet over medium-high heat. Add the filet mignon steaks and cook for 2-3 minutes on each side, or until browned and cooked to your desired level of doneness. Remove the steaks from the skillet and set aside.
3. In the same skillet, add sliced mushrooms and minced garlic. Cook until the mushrooms are golden brown and tender.
4. Deglaze the skillet with white wine, scraping up any browned bits from the bottom. Let the wine reduce slightly.
5. Stir in heavy cream and chopped parsley. Simmer for a few minutes until the sauce thickens.
6. Return the cooked filet mignon steaks to the skillet, coating them with the mushroom cream sauce.
7. Serve the filet mignon escalopes hot, garnished with additional chopped parsley if desired.

Chapter (15) Filet Mignon Desserts

A. Chocolate Filet Mignon Truffles
Ingredients:

- 8 oz cooked filet mignon, finely chopped
- 8 oz dark chocolate, chopped
- 1/4 cup heavy cream
- Cocoa powder, for coating

Instructions:

1. In a heatproof bowl, combine the chopped filet mignon and chopped dark chocolate.
2. In a small saucepan, heat the heavy cream over medium heat until it just begins to simmer.
3. Pour the hot cream over the chopped filet mignon and chocolate. Let it sit for 1-2 minutes.
4. Stir the mixture until the chocolate is completely melted and smooth.
5. Cover the bowl with plastic wrap and refrigerate for at least 2 hours, or until the mixture is firm.
6. Once the mixture is firm, use a small spoon or melon baller to scoop out portions and roll them into small truffles.
7. Roll the truffles in cocoa powder to coat.
8. Store the truffles in an airtight container in the refrigerator until ready to serve.

B. Filet Mignon Ice Cream (Tongue-in-Cheek)
Ingredients:

- 1 cup cooked filet mignon, chopped into small pieces
- 2 cups heavy cream
- 1 cup whole milk
- 3/4 cup granulated sugar
- 1 teaspoon vanilla extract
- Pinch of salt

Instructions:

1. In a blender or food processor, combine the chopped filet mignon, heavy cream, whole milk, sugar, vanilla extract, and salt.
2. Blend the mixture until smooth and well combined.
3. Transfer the mixture to an ice cream maker and churn according to the manufacturer's instructions until it reaches a soft-serve consistency.
4. If desired, fold in additional chopped filet mignon pieces for texture.
5. Transfer the churned ice cream to a freezer-safe container and freeze for at least 4 hours, or until firm.
6. Serve the filet mignon ice cream scoops in dessert bowls or cones for a truly unique and unexpected dessert experience.

Chapter (16) Preserving and Repurposing Filet Mignon

A. Freezing and Reheating Tips

1. Freezing Filet Mignon: To freeze cooked filet mignon, allow it to cool completely first. Then, wrap individual portions tightly in plastic wrap or aluminum foil to prevent freezer burn. Place the wrapped portions in a freezer-safe container or resealable plastic bag, removing as much air as possible before sealing. Label the container with the date and store it in the freezer for up to 3 months.

2. Reheating Frozen Filet Mignon: When ready to reheat frozen filet mignon, thaw it overnight in the refrigerator. Once thawed, you can reheat it using various methods:

3. Oven: Preheat the oven to 350°F (175°C), place the filet mignon on a baking sheet, and reheat for 10-15 minutes, or until warmed through.

4. Stovetop: Heat a skillet over medium heat, add a small amount of oil or butter, and sear the filet mignon for a few minutes on each side until heated through.

5. Sous Vide: Place the frozen filet mignon in a vacuum-sealed bag and cook it in a sous vide water bath at 130°F (54°C) for 45-60 minutes, or until warmed to the desired temperature.

B. Using Filet Mignon in Leftover Makeovers

1. Filet Mignon Stir-Fry: Slice leftover filet mignon thinly and stir-fry it with vegetables such as bell peppers, onions, and broccoli. Add your favorite stir-fry sauce and serve over rice or noodles for a quick and flavorful meal.

2. Filet Mignon Salad: Slice leftover filet mignon and serve it over

a bed of mixed greens with toppings such as cherry tomatoes, cucumbers, avocado, and crumbled cheese. Drizzle with your favorite salad dressing for a light and refreshing meal.

3. Filet Mignon Sandwiches: Thinly slice leftover filet mignon and use it to make sandwiches or wraps with your favorite toppings and condiments. Add lettuce, tomato, onion, and mayonnaise for a classic steak sandwich.

C. Canning and Preserving Filet Mignon for Longevity

Canning and preserving filet mignon is not a common practice due to its delicate texture and flavor. However, you can utilize techniques like pressure canning to preserve cooked filet mignon in dishes such as stews or soups. Here's a general outline:

1. Prepare the Filet Mignon Dish: Cook filet mignon in a flavorful broth or sauce, such as beef broth with vegetables, to create a hearty stew or soup.
2. Pressure Canning: Ladle the hot filet mignon dish into clean, sterilized canning jars, leaving appropriate headspace according to the canning instructions. Wipe the jar rims clean, place lids and bands on the jars, and tighten until fingertip tight.
3. Process the Jars: Process the filled jars in a pressure canner according to the recommended processing time and pressure for your altitude and the type of food being canned. Follow proper canning procedures and guidelines to ensure safety.
4. Cool and Store: After processing, remove the jars from the pressure canner and let them cool completely. Check the seals to ensure they are airtight, then label the jars with the date and contents before storing them in a cool, dark place for long-term storage.

Chapter (17) Filet Mignon Cooking Challenges

A. Overcoming Tough Cuts and Grains

1. Selecting Quality Cuts: Choose filet mignon cuts with consistent marbling and minimal connective tissue for tenderness. Look for well-trimmed steaks with even thickness to ensure uniform cooking.
2. Tenderizing Techniques: Consider using tenderizing methods such as marinating in acidic ingredients like citrus juice or vinegar, or using a meat mallet to gently pound the steak to break down muscle fibers.

B. Addressing Flavor Fatigue

1. Variety in Seasonings: Experiment with different seasonings, rubs, and marinades to add variety and depth of flavor to your filet mignon. Try incorporating herbs, spices, garlic, or citrus zest for a fresh twist.
2. Incorporate Sauces and Accompaniments: Pair filet mignon with flavorful sauces or accompaniments such as compound butters, mushroom sauces, or tangy chimichurri to enhance its taste and combat flavor fatigue.

C. Experimenting with Unconventional Cooking Methods

1. Sous Vide Cooking: Try cooking filet mignon using the sous vide method for precise temperature control and consistent results. Sous vide cooking involves vacuum-sealing the steak and immersing it in a water bath at a precise temperature until it reaches the desired level of doneness.
2. Smoking or Grilling: Experiment with smoking or grilling filet

mignon for a unique flavor profile. Use wood chips or charcoal to infuse the steak with smoky aromas, enhancing its taste and texture.

D. Managing Filet Mignon's Sensitivity to Overcooking

1. Use a Meat Thermometer: Invest in a reliable meat thermometer to accurately gauge the internal temperature of the filet mignon. This ensures that you cook the steak to your desired level of doneness without the risk of overcooking.
2. Resting Period: Allow the cooked filet mignon to rest for a few minutes before slicing or serving. This allows the juices to redistribute throughout the meat, resulting in a more tender and flavorful steak.

E. Troubleshooting Temperature Fluctuations

1. Preheat Cooking Surface: Ensure that your cooking surface, whether it's a grill, skillet, or oven, is properly preheated before cooking filet mignon. This helps maintain consistent heat and prevents temperature fluctuations during cooking.
2. Monitor Cooking Environment: Be mindful of external factors such as wind, humidity, or fluctuations in ambient temperature, which can affect cooking times and temperatures. Make adjustments as needed to maintain optimal cooking conditions.

Chapter (18) Filet Mignon for Entertaining

A. Hosting a Filet Mignon Dinner Party

1. Menu Planning: Plan a luxurious menu featuring filet mignon as the centerpiece. Offer a variety of sides, sauces, and accompaniments to complement the steak, such as roasted vegetables, mashed potatoes, and red wine reduction sauce.
2. Table Setting: Set an elegant table with fine linens, dinnerware, and candlelight to create a sophisticated ambiance for your dinner party.
3. Interactive Cooking: Consider incorporating interactive elements into the dinner party, such as a DIY steak seasoning station or a live cooking demonstration where guests can learn how to cook the perfect filet mignon.

B. Creating Filet Mignon Charcuterie Boards

1. Selection of Ingredients: Assemble a charcuterie board featuring thinly sliced filet mignon alongside an assortment of cured meats, cheeses, crackers, bread, olives, nuts, and fruits.
2. Garnishes and Accompaniments: Enhance the presentation of the charcuterie board with fresh herbs, mustard, honey, fig jam, and pickled vegetables to complement the flavors of the filet mignon.
3. Customization: Offer a variety of options for guests to customize their charcuterie experience, such as different types of cheese and condiments, to cater to individual tastes.

C. Incorporating Filet Mignon into Tapas Nights

1. Small Bites: Prepare bite-sized filet mignon dishes such as filet

mignon skewers, sliders, or crostini to serve as part of a tapas-style menu.

2. Variety of Flavors: Offer a diverse selection of tapas dishes featuring different flavors and textures to complement the richness of the filet mignon, such as seafood, vegetables, and Spanish-inspired appetizers.

3. Sharing Plates: Arrange the tapas dishes on sharing plates or platters for guests to enjoy together, encouraging social interaction and conversation.

D. Interactive Cooking Stations Featuring Filet Mignon

1. Grilling Station: Set up a grilling station where guests can grill their own filet mignon steaks to their preferred level of doneness. Provide a variety of seasonings, marinades, and sauces for guests to customize their steak.

2. Sous Vide Station: Create a sous vide cooking station where guests can experience the sous vide cooking method by vacuum-sealing and cooking filet mignon in a water bath. Offer different cooking times and temperatures for guests to experiment with.

3. Accompaniments Bar: Set up a toppings and accompaniments bar with a variety of sauces, compound butters, and garnishes for guests to personalize their filet mignon dishes.

E. Filet Mignon Pairings with Appetizers and Desserts

1. Appetizer Pairings: Serve filet mignon appetizers such as bacon-wrapped filet mignon bites or filet mignon crostini paired with complementary appetizers such as stuffed mushrooms, bruschetta, or shrimp cocktail.

2. Dessert Pairings: Pair filet mignon with indulgent desserts such as chocolate lava cake, berry tarts, or crème brûlée for a sweet and savory contrast that will impress your guests.

Chapter (19) Sustainable Filet Mignon Practices

A. Understanding the Environmental Impact of Filet Mignon Production

1. Resource Intensiveness: Recognize that traditional methods of producing filet mignon, particularly those associated with industrialized farming practices, can have significant environmental impacts. These include land use, water consumption, greenhouse gas emissions, and deforestation.

2. Carbon Footprint: Understand that beef production, including filet mignon, contributes to greenhouse gas emissions, primarily methane, and carbon dioxide. This is due to factors such as cattle feed, transportation, and manure management.

B. Ethical Sourcing and Responsible Consumption

1. Grass-Fed and Pasture-Raised Options: Choose filet mignon from producers that prioritize sustainable and ethical farming practices. Look for labels indicating grass-fed, pasture-raised, or certified organic beef, which often have lower environmental impacts compared to conventional feedlot operations.

2. Certifications and Standards: Support producers who adhere to third-party certifications and standards for animal welfare, environmental sustainability, and ethical labor practices, such as Certified Humane, Animal Welfare Approved, or USDA Organic.

C. Supporting Local Farms and Butchers

1. Locally Sourced Filet Mignon: Purchase filet mignon from local farms and butchers whenever possible. By supporting local

producers, you reduce the environmental footprint associated with transportation and distribution, while also contributing to the local economy.

2. Direct Relationships: Establish direct relationships with local farmers and butchers to learn more about their farming practices, animal welfare standards, and environmental initiatives. This transparency can help you make informed choices about the filet mignon you consume.

D. Reducing Food Waste with Filet Mignon

1. Portion Control: Practice portion control when serving filet mignon to avoid overestimating the amount needed for a meal. Consider serving smaller portion sizes and complementing the dish with a variety of side dishes and accompaniments to create a satisfying meal.

2. Leftover Utilization: Repurpose leftover filet mignon into new dishes such as stir-fries, salads, or sandwiches to minimize food waste. Freeze leftover cooked filet mignon for future use in soups, stews, or casseroles.

E. Exploring Alternative Protein Sources

1. Plant-Based Alternatives: Incorporate plant-based protein sources such as beans, lentils, tofu, tempeh, or seitan into your diet as alternatives to filet mignon. Plant-based proteins generally have a lower environmental impact compared to animal products and can contribute to a more sustainable diet.

2. Seafood Options: Include sustainably sourced seafood options such as wild-caught fish or shellfish in your meals as alternatives to beef. Choose seafood that is certified by reputable organizations such as the Marine Stewardship Council (MSC) or the Aquaculture Stewardship Council (ASC).

Chapter (20) Filet Mignon Garnishes and Flair

A. Fresh Herb Arrangements for Plating

1. Herb Bouquets: Create herb bouquets using a variety of fresh herbs such as rosemary, thyme, sage, and parsley. Tie them together with kitchen twine and place them alongside or on top of the cooked filet mignon for a vibrant and aromatic presentation.
2. Herb Sprinkles: Finely chop fresh herbs and sprinkle them over the plated filet mignon just before serving. This adds a burst of color and freshness to the dish, enhancing both the visual appeal and flavor profile.

B. Edible Flower Accents

1. Petals and Blossoms: Use edible flowers such as pansies, nasturtiums, violets, or rose petals to garnish filet mignon dishes. Arrange the flowers delicately on the plate or scatter them around the steak for a visually stunning presentation.
2. Floral Infusions: Incorporate floral flavors into sauces or garnishes to complement the filet mignon. Infuse vinegars or syrups with edible flowers like lavender or hibiscus for a unique and elegant touch.

C. Infused Oils and Vinegars

1. Flavored Oils: Drizzle filet mignon with infused oils such as garlic-infused olive oil, truffle-infused oil, or chili-infused oil for added depth of flavor and richness.
2. Balsamic Reductions: Create decorative swirls or drizzles of balsamic reduction around the plate for an elegant

presentation. Experiment with flavored balsamic reductions such as fig or raspberry for unique flavor combinations.

D. Decorative Vegetable Carvings

1. Vegetable Ribbons: Use a vegetable peeler to create thin ribbons of colorful vegetables such as carrots, zucchini, or beets. Arrange the ribbons in intricate patterns or twists on the plate to add visual interest and texture.
2. Vegetable Flowers: Carve vegetables such as radishes, cucumbers, or bell peppers into decorative flower shapes using small cookie cutters or carving tools. Place the vegetable flowers around the plate as decorative accents for a creative presentation.

E. Artful Sauces and Drizzles

1. Sauce Swirls: Use a squeeze bottle or spoon to create elegant swirls or patterns with sauces such as béarnaise, red wine reduction, or mushroom sauce on the plate. This adds visual flair and enhances the presentation of the filet mignon.
2. Flavorful Drizzles: Drizzle filet mignon with flavorful sauces or reductions such as herb-infused butter, demi-glace, or truffle aioli for a finishing touch that enhances the overall taste and presentation of the dish.

❖ Conclusion

A. Final Thoughts

In conclusion, mastering the art of filet mignon opens up a world of culinary possibilities. This tender and flavorful cut of beef has captivated the palates of food enthusiasts for generations, and with good reason. Whether enjoyed as a classic steak dinner, incorporated into innovative recipes, or showcased as part of an elaborate meal, filet mignon never fails to impress.

B. Encouragement for Culinary Exploration with Filet Mignon

As you embark on your culinary journey with filet mignon, I encourage you to embrace experimentation and creativity. Don't be afraid to explore new cooking techniques, flavor combinations, and presentation styles. Whether you're hosting a dinner party, cooking for your family, or simply treating yourself to a special meal, filet mignon offers endless opportunities for culinary exploration and expression.

Remember to prioritize quality and sustainability in your sourcing practices, support local producers and ethical farming practices, and minimize food waste whenever possible. By making conscious choices and embracing a spirit of culinary adventure, you can savor the joy of cooking and sharing delicious meals with loved ones.

C. Resources for Further Learning and Inspiration

To further expand your knowledge and skills in cooking with filet mignon, consider exploring the following resources:

1. Cookbooks: Explore cookbooks dedicated to beef and steak recipes, as well as those focused specifically on filet mignon. Look for titles authored by renowned chefs and experts in the field for inspiration and guidance.

2. Online Communities: Join online forums, social media groups, and culinary communities dedicated to cooking and food enthusiasts. Engage with fellow home cooks, share your

experiences, and exchange recipe ideas and tips for cooking filet mignon.

3. Cooking Classes and Workshops: Attend cooking classes or workshops focused on beef cookery and steak preparation. Many culinary schools, cooking academies, and community centers offer classes covering various cooking techniques and methods for preparing filet mignon.

4. Farmers Markets and Butcher Shops: Visit local farmers markets and butcher shops to connect with producers and learn more about different cuts of beef, including filet mignon. Ask questions, seek recommendations, and explore the diverse selection of high-quality meats available.

www.ingramcontent.com/pod-product-compliance
Lightning Source LLC
Chambersburg PA
CBHW060501160726
47992CB00003B/1281